S0-FQV-269

THE TEFILLIN HANDBOOK

Dovid Rosoff

THE
TEFILLIN
HANDBOOK

*A Practical Guide
based on Talmudic sources
and the Mishna Berura*

FELDHEIM PUBLISHERS
Jerusalem / New York

edited by Shimon Hurwitz

graphics by Shmuel Gluck (and Craig Ehrlich)

photography by Donn Gross, D.R.

illustration by I.A. Kaufman

First published 1984
ISBN 0-87306-373-2

Copyright © 1984 by
Dovid Rosoff

All rights reserved

No part of this publication may be translated,
reproduced, stored in a retrieval system or transmitted,
in any form or by any means,
electronic, mechanical, photocopying, recording or otherwise,
without prior permission in writing from the publishers

Philipp Feldheim Inc.
200 Airport Executive Park
Spring Valley, NY 10977

96 East Broadway
New York, NY 10002

Feldheim Publishers Ltd
POB 6525 / Jerusalem, Israel

Printed in Israel

Contents

והאר עינינו בתורתך ודבק לבנו במצותיך ויחד לבבנו לאהבה ולראה את שמך...

רב ונשיא
הג׳ ר׳ משה שטרנבוך שליט״א
ראש בעורי הרבנים (נ׳א) ועוד׳

RAV & DIRECTOR
RABBI MOISHE STERNBUCH

P.O. BOX 3131
JOHANNESBURG 2000
REP. OF SOUTH AFRICA.
TELEPHONE
(011) 648-5374

to hear, to learn, to teach
לשמע ללמד וללמד

Dear Rabbi Rossoff נ״י,

I have received your booklet on Tephilin, which has already been recommended by Rabbinical Authorities in Jerusalem. I have read it through, and I feel sure the English speaking public will derive great benefit from this handbook which I strongly recommend.

You have succeeded to explain in simple language the essence of the Mitzvah, and through accepting advice from Rabbis in all doubtful cases, you have assured yourself בע״ה that you will succeed in your motives.

I feel sure that your booklet will impress on readers the importance to lay Tephilin every day, and to observe the Mitzvah according to the Laws as set up in *Shulchan Aruch*.

Accept my blessings, you should succeed in your work as through the Mitzvah of Tephilin we will sanctify the name of G-d and be blessed with complete redemption.

Best Wishes
Moishe Sternbuch

RABBI MOSES FEINSTEIN		משה פיינשטיין
455 F. D. R. DRIVE		ר"מ תפארת ירושלים
New York, N. Y. 10002		בנוא יארק
—		
ORegon 7-1222		בע"ה

הנה קבלתי הקונטרס על הלכות תפילין שחיברו הרה"ג מוהר"ר דוד
רוסאף שליט"א. קונטרס זה נכתב באנגלית, ומסרתיו לנכדי, הרה"ג
מוהר"ר מרדכי סנדלר שליט"א, שעיין בו, ושיבחו כספר שיכול להיות
לתועלת לאלו שמתחילים ללמוד הלכות אלו, מאחר שנכתב בלשון בהיר
ונסדר באופן משכלת. והספר כולל גם מראה מקומות ארוכות, שיעיין
גם אלו שרוצים להעמיק יותר בהלכות אלו.

והרידני מברך להמחבר הנ"ל שיצליחהו השי"ת בספרו זה, ויזכה ע"י
להרבות ידיעות התורה.

ועל זה באתי על החתום בכ"ד אדר שני שדמ"ת בנוא יארק.

משה פיינשטיין

I received the booklet on the laws of *tefillin* written by David Rosoff.
As this booklet is written in English, I gave it to my grandson, the
learned Rabbi Mordechai Tendler, who examined it, and praised it
as a work that can be useful to persons beginning to learn these
laws, since it is written in clear language and arranged in an
intelligent manner. The work includes lengthy references as well,
which will be of interest to those who wish to delve further into these
laws.

I hereby bless the author, that HaShem may give him success
with this work; and may he be privileged to increase by it a
knowledge of the Torah.

To this I have set my name, on 24 Adar II, 5744, in New York.

Vaad Mishmereth Stam

וַעַד מִשְׁמֶרֶת סתּ״ם

The center for international activities to preserve and promote the halachic integrity
of scribal arts: Torah Scrolls, Tefillin And Mezuzos

Rosh Chodesh Teveth 5744

How truly pleased and happy we are at seeing the new publication, **The Tefillin Handbook**, the fruitful work of Rabbi David Rossoff, שליט״א, who has worked diligently and tirelessly to bring merit to the Jewish people through this important book, as it is testified to by great rabbinical authorities in their recommendations.

Concerning STAM, in general, and mitzvath tefillin, in particular, as great as their lofty holiness and as cherished as they are to our people, unfortunately there is no measure to the fraudulent pitfalls which exist in this holy area. Many people throughout the world are being misled, as it is known, "the greater the holiness, the greater the likelihood of destroying such holiness." The problem applies not only to the *halachoth* of proper writing and formation of the letters, whose *kashruth* is by a hairbreadth, but also to other important *halachoth* of tefillin such as *batim, retzuoth*, proper binding on the arm and head, and so forth.

From experience, we are certain that our fellow Jews wear tefillin with the sole desire of performing the mitzvah as required but fail in this goal simply because they lack sufficient knowledge of the *halachoth*. And, therefore, it is fitting to give respect and esteem to the author, Rabbi David Rossoff, who felt impelled to deal with this important mitzvah. And how great is his merit (see *Sefer Chassidim*, section 65), because increasing the knowledge of these *halachoth* will promote the diligence and carefulness with which this mitzvah is performed and, thereby, will remove great disgrace from the Jewish people.

In this merit, may we be deserving of all the Torah blessings and promises that are mentioned concerning the mitzvah of tefillin, and may we see fulfilled in us, as it is stated, "And all the peoples of the earth will see that the Name of Hashem is called upon you and they shall be in awe of you."

בכבוד רב הברכה

4902 16th Avenue, Brooklyn, N.Y. 11204   Phone: (212) 438-4963

ACTIVITIES: PUBLIC EDUCATION: AUDIO/VISUAL PRESENTATIONS / PUBLICATIONS / EXHIBITIONS ● EDUCATIONAL PROGRAMS FOR SCHOOLS AND SYNA
● CONSUMER PROTECTION SERVICE ● EXAMINATION LABORATORY ● COMMUNITY MEZUZOS AND TEFILLIN EXAMINATION CAMPAIGNS ● YESHIVA FOR SOFRIM
LAWS OF STAM ● VOCATIONAL INSTITUTE FOR PROFESSIONAL SCRIBES AND EXAMINERS ● HALACHIC RESEARCH INSTITUTE: DIVISION OF SEPHARDIC TRADITI
CUSTOMS ● ENCYCLOPEDIA AND DIGEST OF THE SACRED ALPHABET FOR SCHOLARS AND LAYMEN

PREFACE

Tefillin has the potential to bind body and soul to the Creator. But as a minimum, we must fulfill one essential condition: that we know we are putting on tefillin. If this prerequisite is not fulilled, the tefillin become no more than "boxes of stone," *chas v'shalom* (see *Aterath Zekenim* 25:2).

Therefore, in order both to assist the novice and to provide a quick review for others, this handbook has been prepared for the benefit of the Torah public.

In it, three areas of *hilchoth* tefillin have been tied together. First, the practical *halacha l'maaseh* is set down with its reference in the *Mishna Berura* and *poskim*. Second, the Talmudic source of the *halacha* is discussed side by side with the *halacha*. And thirdly, relevant stories and reasons for the *halacha* have also been included.

It is hoped that this "tripled-stranded cord" will help dispell areas of ignorance and make certain that we are wearing tefillin and not "boxes of stone."

THIRTEEN-POINT QUESTIONNAIRE

First we want you, our reader, to test your knowledge on tefillin, and then we will give the answers. Put a check by each question where you know the answer. After you finish this handbook, come back again and make sure that you know the answers to all the questions.

[1] What do the words "tefillin" and "*totofoth*" mean? What do they tell us about the meaning of wearing tefillin?

[2] How many times is the mitzvah of tefillin mentioned in the Torah? Where? Why?

[3] What is the difference in the order of the *parshiyoth* between Rashi and Rabbenu Tam?

[4] Why does a right-handed person bind tefillin on his left arm, and a left-handed person, on his right arm? Why is the *shel yad* placed on the biceps muscle of the arm and not, as the *posuk* says, "as a sign upon your *hand*"? (*Devorim* 6:8).

[5] Why do we place the *shel rosh* above the forehead and

not, as the *posuk* states, "as frontlets between your eyes"? (Ibid.)

[6] Why are tefillin perfectly square? Why must they be black? What material are they made from and why?

[7] Why does the *shel yad* have one compartment for all the *parshiyoth* while the *shel rosh* has four separate compartments?

[8] Why is the *shel yad* put on first and the *shel rosh* taken off first?

[9] How many *berachoth* are made? Must one stand when putting on tefillin?

[10] Are the straps of the tefillin absolutely necessary? Must they also be black? How many times is the strap wound around the arm? The permanent knots of the *shel rosh* and the *shel yad* look like which Hebrew letters?

[11] What are the *titura* and the *ma'abarta*?

[12] Can tefillin be worn at night? Why are they not worn on Shabbat and Yom Tov? When are tefillin first worn?

[13] Why is the letter *shin* found only on the *shel rosh*? How many times? Can it be simply painted on? Why does one *shin* have four heads?

ANSWERS WITH EXPLANATION

[1] WHAT DO THE WORDS "TEFILLIN" AND "TOTOFOTH" MEAN? WHAT DO THEY TELL US ABOUT THE MEANING OF WEARING TEFILLIN?

According to most commentators, the word "tefillin" comes from the Hebrew word *pilel*, [פילל], which can mean either to argue, "And Pinchas stood up and argued [ויפלל]" (*Tehillim* 106:30), or to think out clearly, as in the *posuk*, "I had not thought [פללתי] to see your face" (*Bereishith* 48:11).[1]

The word *totofoth*, referring to the tefillin *shel rosh*, means headband and is often translated "frontlets."[2]

In what ways do these definitions help us to understand better the mitzvah of wearing tefillin?

First, tefillin represent a visible proof and testimony to the world that the Name of HaShem is placed on the Jewish People. By publicly wearing these frontlets, for no other reason than to fulfill HaShem's commandments, we are dramatically arguing HaShem's absolute rulership. Thereby, we show ourselves as His only true and obedient servants, receiving the awe and respect due His representatives. This is the meaning of the *posuk*, "And all the peoples of the earth shall see that the Name of the L-rd is called upon you; and they shall be afraid of you."[3]

Second, tefillin tell us the central role of thinking in the Jewish way of life. Concentration, meditation, memorization are essential when the Jew prays and learns Torah.[4] The tefillin *shel rosh* shows the requirement of bringing the reasoning powers of the brain closer to the service of HaShem. The tefillin *shel yad* opposite the heart indicates the need for controlling passionate thoughts, for example, anger, greed, lust.

Third, tefillin remind us to *think* about our Divine mission in the world. The four *parshiyoth* inside the tefillin represent the four letters of HaShem's Name[5] and define four basic components of our Jewish existence:

(a)Total acceptance of the yoke of the Kingdom of Heaven [Love of HaShem].[6]

(b)Total acceptance of all the commandments of HaShem [Fear of HaShem].[7]

(c)Complete dedication of all material possessions to the service of HaShem [self-sacrifice].[8]

(d)Absolute realization that HaShem controls all of nature and the events of man [the Exodus from Egypt].[9]

Now we can understand why someone who recites the *Shema* without putting tefillin on is compared to a witness who gives false testimony.[10] For tefillin are the physical representation of the words which we are speaking and thinking about, and it would be false to mention the requirement of wearing tefillin and not put them on.

Fourth, we can also define tefillin in the sense of arguing or pleading our cause before HaShem.[11] "See that we are wearing tefillin and please accept our prayers – even if we have shortcomings. Our desire to do Your will is expressed at this very moment as we wear Your mitzvah of tefillin. So, though we ourselves may have no merits, may the tefillin plead [פליל] our cause and give us the merit to have our prayers answered."

[2] HOW MANY TIMES IS THE MITZVAH OF TEFILLIN MENTIONED IN THE TORAH? WHERE? WHY?

Tefillin are mentioned four times in the Torah:

1) קדש *Kadesh* (*Shemoth* 13:1-10).
2) והיה כי יביאך *V'haya ki yevi'acha* (Ibid. 13:11-16).
3) שמע ישראל *Shema Yisroel* (*Devorim* 6:4-9).
4) והיה אם שמע *V'haya im shamoah* (Ibid. 11:13-21).

These same four *parshiyoth* are placed in both the tefillin *shel rosh* and the tefillin *shel yad* as we partially discussed in the question before. The *Shema* and *V'haya im shamoah* we say in the *Kiriyath Shema* of *Shacharith*, and it is a good custom to say the other two, either right after putting on the tefillin or after *davening*, before removing the tefillin.[12]

The *Shema* describes the Oneness of HaShem and our desire to join with that Oneness even until death. This *parsha* is called "accepting the yoke of the Kingdom of Heaven" and is an intense expression of our undying love of HaShem. By studying

Torah wholeheartedly, we form an inseparable closeness to HaShem, as it says, "...and you shall speak of them,"[13] that is, by constantly learning Torah the Oneness of HaShem will become more a part of you. Further, when we check through all the mitzvoth, we discover that tefillin more than any other mitzvah implants in us the full scope of learning Torah, as the *posuk* says, "so that the Torah of HaShem shall be in your mouth."[14]

Rabbenu Yona also explains that tefillin are an expression of our acceptance of the Almighty's Kingship since the *shel rosh* shows our willingness to submit our minds to Him, and the *shel yad* shows our willingness to subjugate our bodily actions to His will.[15]

While the *Shema* expresses the love of HaShem, *V'haya im shamoah* teaches fear of HaShem by describing the rewards for doing the mitzvoth and the punishments for failing to do them. Tefillin represent the obligation to fulfill *all* of HaShem's mitzvoth since many mitzvoth directly or indirectly relate to the mitzvah of tefillin – for example, studying Torah [the *Shema* must be read with tefillin on], eating kosher animals [only the skin of kosher animals may be used to make tefillin], and believing in the Oral Tradition [that the straps must be black] and the wisdom of *Chazal* [not to wear tefillin at night].

Further, we see in this *parsha* that the stress is changed from the singular to the plural in order to teach us that the Jewish community as a whole is also responsible for keeping HaShem's mitzvoth. How wonderful it is to see this joint responsibility in action when, for example, one Jew is helping another to put on tefillin!

The last two *parshiyoth, Kadesh* and *V'haya ki yevi'acha,* appear strange and unrelated to tefillin. What does redeeming the firstborn have to do with tefillin? How do the Exodus and the mitzvah of *Pesach* and the *Haggadah* fit into the mitzvah of tefillin? Rabbi Hirsch explains[16] that when the firstborn were set apart to act as priests of the Jewish People,[17] a misunderstanding might have occurred, namely, that just the firstborn were holy and not the rest of the Jewish People. Therefore, when Moshe gave over the mitzvah of the firstborn, he reminded everybody of the Exodus – which equally freed everybody from bondage and equally brought them all into freedom. Further, he mentioned the significance of transmitting the freedom to everybody – as we do by reading the *Haggadah* on the *Seder* night – which shows that everyone has an equal task in serving HaShem. Finally, Moshe taught them that the mitzvoth – exemplified by tefillin – sanctified everyone equally, but the firstborn were given the additional task of conducting the Temple service.

[3] WHAT IS THE DIFFERENCE IN THE ORDER OF THE *PARSHIYOTH* BETWEEN RASHI AND RABBENU TAM?

What is the order of the *parshiyoth*? Our first guess would be that they are the same order as they appear in the Torah. Indeed,

Rashi understands it that way (see Diagram 1). Rabbenu Tam, however, changes the last two around as can be seen in Diagram 1,[18] but he agrees with Rashi that when writing the four *parshiyoth*, the *sofer* must write them in the order in which they appear in the Torah.

DIAGRAM 1

3	4	2	1	RABBENU TAM
4	3	2	1	RASHI

1   קדש

2   והיה כי יביאך

3   שמע ישראל

4   והיה אם שמע

PLACE WHERE CALF'S HAIR
STICKS OUT
1 – ACCORDING TO RASHI
2 – ACCORDING TO
    RABBENU TAM

Today Rabbenu Tam tefillin are generally worn by Sephar-adim and Chassidim, but because of their high level of holiness, they are not worn until after marriage. Interestingly, some Chassidic groups have the *minhag* of wearing Rabbenu Tam already from the time of Bar Mitzvah. The *berachoth* are made only on the Rashi tefillin which are put on first and not on the Rabbenu Tam tefillin.

It is easy to recognize the *shel rosh* of Rabbenu Tam tefillin: look where the thread of calf's hair sticks out. The accepted *halacha* is that this hair should come out next to the compart-ment containing *V'haya im shamoah*.[19] Since Rashi and Rabbenu Tam disagree over which compartment *V'haya im shamoah* goes into, the calf's hair is located at a different place according to each viewpoint (see insert to Diagram 1).

[4] WHY DOES A RIGHT-HANDED PERSON BIND TEFILLIN ON HIS LEFT ARM, AND A LEFT-HANDED PERSON, ON HIS RIGHT ARM? WHY IS THE *SHEL YAD* PLACED ON THE BICEPS MUSCLE OF THE ARM AND NOT, AS THE *POSUK* SAYS, "AS A SIGN UPON YOUR *HAND*"? (*DEVORIM* 6:8).

When the Torah mentions "hand" without discriminating be-tween right or left hand, it means the left hand. *Chazal* understood this principle because whenever a *posuk* refers to the right hand specifically, it says either "right" or "right hand," as in "Why do You withdraw Your hand, even Your right hand?" (*Tehillim* 74:11).[20]

Another way that *Chazal* explain that the *shel yad* is placed on the left hand is by comparing the *posuk* "you shall bind it as a sign" with the *posuk* that follows it, "...and you shall write it on your doorposts."[21] Just as writing is normally done with the right hand, so also the binding should be done with the right hand. Obviously, then, if the right hand is doing the binding, the tefillin must be placed on the left hand.

There is yet a third method to prove that tefillin are put on the left hand.[22] At the end of *V'haya ki yevi'acha* (*Shemoth* 13:16), "your hand" is spelled with an extra *hei*, יָדְכָה, normally used to show a feminine ending. Here it hints to "your weak(er) hand," which for a right-handed person means his left hand and for a left-handed person, his right hand.[23] Someone who uses both hands equally well, or who writes with one hand though his other hand is stronger, should consult his rabbi.

Now that we know the sources for placing it on the left arm, how do we know to place it on the biceps muscle between the shoulder and the elbow, and not on the forearm between the elbow and the wrist, or on the palm of the hand itself? The *Gemora* discusses the question: "The Academy of Menashe taught:[24] 'Your hand' refers to the biceps muscle." And how do we know this to be true? Rabbi Eliezer gives one explanation:[25] " 'And it shall be for *you* as a sign' – for you, and not for others." If a person wore tefillin on his hand, everybody would see it. However, if he wears tefillin on the upper part of his arm since his shirt would usually cover it, then it is a "sign" only for himself. The *halacha* is that the tefillin *shel yad* does not have to be covered so long as it is on the part of the arm which people normally cover.[26] Still, the better practice is always to cover the tefillin with one's shirt sleeve.[27]

Rabbi Yitzchak offers another method of learning where on the arm the tefillin should be placed.[28] The Torah says, "And you shall lay My words in your heart...and you shall bind them."[29] The binding of the *shel yad* shall be on the arm opposite the heart, that is, on the biceps muscle. From Rabbi Yitzchak's words, we learn that we should tilt the *shel yad* slightly towards the body so that when the arm hangs down, the tefillin (and its *yud*–shaped knot) will be directly opposite the heart[30] (see Diagram 2).

DIAGRAM 2

RIGHT   WRONG

The upper part of the arm is divided roughly into three sections (see Diagram 3). The middle section is the area in which the muscle bulges and is known as the biceps muscle. The proper place for the *shel yad* begins at the *middle* of this area and continues along the bulge towards the direction of the elbow. Higher up than this bulge towards the shoulder should not be used, and very close to the elbow, which is already below the bulge of the biceps muscle, should also not be used.

DIAGRAM 3

However, when there is a wound or bandage on the biceps muscle, tefillin are not allowed to be placed on the bandage but must instead be placed either just below the biceps muscle or, if this area is also wounded, just above the biceps muscle.[31] If these areas also cause discomfort, a rabbi should be consulted whether the *shel yad* is still required.

Although some authorities do not view the tefillin straps as a separation between the tefillin and the flesh of the arm, it is better not to wind the strap under the *bayith* of the *shel yad*.[32]

Why did the Torah seemingly mislead us concerning the proper place for the *shel yad*? In fact, we are warned that anyone who follows the literal words and wears tefillin on the palm of his hand is considered a denier of the Oral Law.[33]

Chazal tell us that the key to fulfilling the mitzvoth is *not* to follow blindly the apparent simple meaning of the written word.[34] Instead, the *Torah she-baal-peh*, which was given hand-in-hand with the Written Law on *Har Sinai*, is our life-line to truth. Therefore, those who do not accept the teaching of our *chachamim* who received it in a direct chain from Moshe Rabbenu are cutting off this life-line and deny our most basic principles. Tefillin affirm our belief in the Oral Tradition and the *chachamim* who conveyed it from the generations before to our own generation.

[5] WHY DO WE PLACE THE *SHEL ROSH* ABOVE THE FOREHEAD AND NOT, AS THE *POSUK* STATES, "AS FRONTLETS BETWEEN YOUR EYES"? (*DEVORIM* 6:8).

Chazal teach that the correct position of the tefillin *shel rosh* is *completely* on the hair at the front of the head and extends backward about half the length of the head.[35] We fulfill the requirement that the tefillin be "between your eyes" by being certain to center it in the middle of the head, directly *above* the point between the eyes (see Diagram 4).

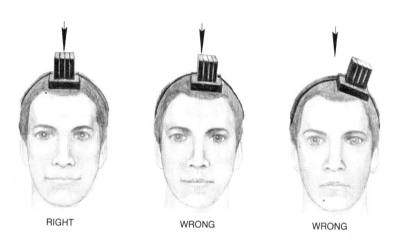

RIGHT   WRONG   WRONG

DIAGRAM 4

Chazal explain that the tefillin *shel rosh* is not placed directly between the eyes because of a *gezerah shava*, a comparison of laws based on the same wording in two places.[36] The words "between your eyes" appear in *Devorim* 14:1 where the prohibition against making a baldness between your eyes is mentioned. Making a baldness as a sign of mourning refers to pulling out the hair on the top of the head. From here, therefore, we understand that with tefillin the expression "between your eyes" means the place on the top of the head.

Special care should be taken to be sure that the *shel rosh* is always in its proper place.[37] Some people use a small pocket mirror to check if the tefillin is perfectly centered while others will ask a friend to see if their *shel rosh* is correctly positioned.[38] It is highly recommended to touch both the *shel yad* and the *shel rosh* regularly, except during the *Shemone Esre,*[39] in order that you should not forget that you are wearing tefillin [היסח הדעת].[40] With your right hand, first touch the *shel yad* and then the *shel rosh*. Further, during the *Kiriyath Shema*, touch the *shel yad* when saying "You shall bind them for a sign on your hand" and the *shel rosh* when saying "as frontlets between your eyes."

There is a famous story in the *Gemora* that took place during a discussion on the tefillin *shel rosh*.[40a] Pilimo asked Rabbi Yehuda HaNassi: "On which head does a two-headed man put on tefillin?" Rebbi was upset at such an absurd question. "Either you leave my presence and go into exile," he ordered, "or else consider yourself under a ban of excommunication." At that moment, a man entered the yeshiva to ask a question regarding the redemption of his firstborn son. "My wife just gave birth to a baby boy with two heads. How many shekel coins do I have to give to the kohen, five as the Torah commands because he is one child, or ten, that is, five for each head?"

Actually, Pilimo was asking a very basic question concerning our *Avodath HaShem*: what parts of our complex mind are we to bring into the service of HaShem?[41] The two heads represent two types of thoughts, one worldly and one heavenly. Pilimo wanted to know if while wearing tefillin a person has both worldly and heavenly matters on his mind, which one should he subjugate to HaShem? Rabbi Yehuda HaNassi reacted sternly because to him the answer was obvious – both types of thoughts have to be turned completely over to the service of HaShem.

The *Mishna Berura* (*Orech Chaim* 27:9 [33]) writes that many people are mistaken about the correct position of the *shel rosh* and say that the edge of the *bayith* (that is, the *ma'abarta*)[42] must touch the hair-line, but the *bayith* itself should lie on the forehead between the eyes. They, in fact, are the ones who are not fulfilling any mitzvah at all. Therefore, one should be extremely careful that all the *bayith*, including the *titura*[42] (base), lies on the hair of the head (see Diagram 5). And best of all, continues the *Mishna Berura*, is to place it slightly further back on the head away from the hair-line to guard against it accidentally sliding forward onto the forehead.

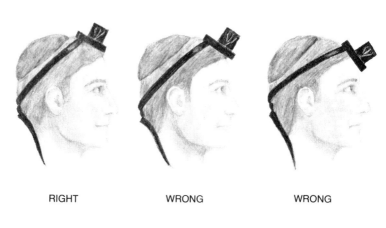

RIGHT   WRONG   WRONG

DIAGRAM 5

A person whose hair-line forms a "widow's peak" must move his tefillin back far enough so that all of it rests on his hair and not part on his hair and part on his forehead (see Diagram 6).

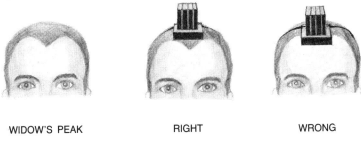

WIDOW'S PEAK   RIGHT   WRONG

DIAGRAM 6

Hair which slopes down slightly onto the forehead does not make the forehead a "free parking zone" for the *shel rosh*. The hair-line is determined by the roots of the hair and not its ends. In addition, long locks of hair lift the tefillin up away from the scalp and cause two problems.[43] First, it is more difficult to keep the *shel rosh* set exactly in the middle of the head because it is resting on an unstable layer of thick hair. And second, some authorities hold that such hair is a separation between the tefillin and the head since it cannot be claimed that long hair is its natural length. Practically speaking, someone with long hair should at least brush the hair down and not backward in order to avoid this problem.[43a]

The *shel rosh* is also called by the name *kanfe yona* (dove wings) because of the famous story that happened to Elisha.[44] The wicked Roman Empire forbade — on penalty of death —

anyone from wearing tefillin. The decree, however, did not alter Elisha's serving his Creator, and he continued wearing his tefillin even publicly. Once, when a Roman officer saw him with his tefillin on, Elisha ran away as the officer chased after him. When Elisha realized that he was going to be overtaken by the officer, he stopped and took off his *shel rosh* and held it tightly in his hand.

"What's that in your hand?" snarled the officer viciously.

Elisha stood his ground and simply replied, "Kanfe yona."

"Let me see," ordered the Roman.

Elisha stretched forth and opened his hand, revealing a dove.

For this reason he was called Elisha *Baal Kanfayim* ("Elisha, the possessor of wings").

(See Photographs, p.34 for three *kanfe yona* ways of wrapping the straps of the *shel rosh*.)

[6] WHY ARE TEFILLIN PERFECTLY SQUARE? WHY MUST THEY BE BLACK? WHAT MATERIAL ARE THEY MADE FROM AND WHY?

Halacha l'Moshe m'Sinai requires that both the *shel yad* and the *shel rosh* be perfectly square. This rule applies to both the *titura* (base) and the stitching that uses twelve holes which, when sewn together, hold the bottom flap of the *titura* flush against the top flap (see Diagram 10).

To ensure that a perfect square is made, the two diagonals (A–A, B–B) must be identical in length and at 90° angles, thereby making the sides of the *titura* (A–B, B–A) equal to each other (see Diagram 7).

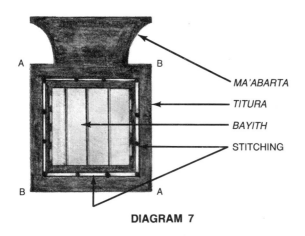

DIAGRAM 7

The sides of the *bayith* (see Diagram 8, a–b) also must be square, but its height (c) does not have to be the same length. In

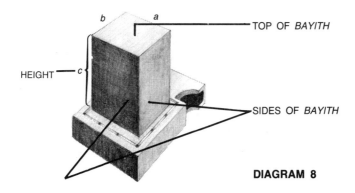

DIAGRAM 8

other words, the *bayith* does not have to be a perfect cube. Since even a slight nick in the sides of the *bayith* may destroy its square shape and make the tefillin *posul*, protective cases are used to store the tefillin. Also, when being worn on the arm under the shirt sleeve, the *shel yad* has another lighter, protective cover, called a *yidel*, which should be removed before reciting the beracha להניח תפילין, and replaced after saying *baruch shem kavod.*[44a] One should slide these coverings on and off very slowly and carefully so that the tefillin do not become damaged.

What in nature is perfectly square? Look around outside. Look around in all the science books. Look here and there, look high and low. Now look again at the tefillin. Amazing! How beautiful! Although it is humanly impossible to make them absolutely square, one thing is certain: they did not fall down from heaven this way.[45] Man, the Jew, made them as perfectly as possible in order to do the will of his Creator.

Both tefillin and their straps are required to be painted black. The black of the straps, however, is a *halacha l'Moshe m'Sinai* while the black of the *bayith* is, according to some authorities, not a Mosaic law.[46] A practical difference occurs when even though black paint chips off the *bayith*, it is still usable when there is no other pair to replace it.

What makes black special from all other colors? Mix any two colors together, and you will always get a third color. Blue with yellow becomes green; green and red become brown; blue and red become purple. Black, however, will not change into any other color in the blending machine. It remains unaffected and unchanged. This special characteristic of tefillin's color hints to the nature of HaShem, for HaShem is unchangeable, as it says, "For I am the L-rd, I do not change" (*Malachi* 3:6).[47]

Why can we not make a pair of tefillin out of cardboard or plastic? They certainly would cost a lot less. The Torah says, "And it [tefillin] shall be for a sign to you upon your hand...that the L-rd's Torah may be in your mouth" (*Shemoth* 13:9). *Chazal* explain that it is permitted to make the tefillin only with what is generally permitted for you to eat – "in your mouth."[48] And it is *halacha l'Moshe m'Sinai* that the material be from the hide of a kosher animal and not from animal bone, or from fish or fowl. However, even though an animal may be prohibited from being eaten because it is a *n'velah* or *t'refeh*, it is still permitted to use its hide to make tefillin.

Since tefillin are made from natural skin and not from wood or plastic, they become part of our body and are not just an artificial badge of honor attached to us. Of course, we have to rise to the occasion by realizing what we are putting on every morning. Perhaps, we should remember that Hashem, as it were, also puts on tefillin every day.[49] Our tefillin describe our relationship with Hashem. Hashem's tefillin describe His relationship with us; for example, one of the inscriptions says, "Who is like Your People Yisroel, one Nation on the earth."[50] We know that Hashem follows His part, but do we fulfill our responsibility?

A metal *shin*-mold used in *gassoth* tefillin.

[7] WHY DOES THE *SHEL YAD* HAVE ONE COMPARTMENT FOR ALL THE *PARSHIYOTH* WHILE THE *SHEL ROSH* HAS FOUR SEPARATE COMPARTMENTS?

The *shel yad* is described by the Torah simply as "a sign upon your hand." *Chazal* note that since the word "sign" is written in the singular and not in the plural, only a single *bayith* is called for.[51] Further, in the same way that it is one sign (one *bayith*) on the outside, so also is it one sign (all written on one long parchment) on the inside.

The *shel rosh* is called *totofoth*, frontlets. In the four *parshiyoth* of tefillin the word *totofoth* appears three times. Rabbi Yishmael says that two of the three times it is written *totofath* טטפת (singular) and once *totofoth* טוטפות (plural).[52] Since the smallest number of any plural is two, he calculated that two (*totofoth*) plus one and one (*totofath*) equal four; therefore, we have four separate compartments.

Rabbi Akiva learns this idea directly from the word *totofoth* [טוטפות], which is a combination of two foreign words, *tat* [טוט] in the Coptic language and *foth* [פות] in the African language. Each word means the number "two," and together they add up to four, indicating the four compartments in the tefillin *shel rosh*.

Adding together these four with the one compartment of the *shel yad*, one has five – symbolic of the five senses.[53] Since the hands are mostly associated with the sense of touch, the *shel yad* represents using this sense and all other actions of the body *l'shem shemayim*. The other four sense organs – the eyes, ears, palate and nose – are located in the head. Consequently, the four compartments of the *shel rosh* indicate the dedication of these four senses to the service of their Creator.

[8] WHY IS THE *SHEL YAD* PUT ON FIRST AND THE *SHEL ROSH* TAKEN OFF FIRST?

The Torah tells us, "You shall bind them [tefillin] for a sign upon your hand and they shall be for frontlets between your eyes" (*Devorim* 6:8). From here we see that the binding on the hand (*shel yad*) is first since it is mentioned first.[54] "They shall be" tells us that as long as the *shel rosh* is between your eyes, "they" both the *shel rosh* and the *shel yad* should be worn. Therefore, we take the *shel rosh* off first so that at no time will the *shel rosh* be worn alone without the *shel yad*.

To assist in following these rules, be sure to take out first the *shel yad* from your tefillin bag and put it on before taking out the *shel rosh*.[55] Only after you have made the beracha and wound the strap down to the wrist, do you then take out the *shel rosh* and put it on your head (see Appendix I, Practical Guide: How to Put on Tefillin, p. 55).

Before taking off the *shel rosh* untie the three windings around the middle finger. The *shel rosh* should be removed with the left hand (weaker hand) to show a reluctance in taking it off.[56] (A left-handed person would use his weaker, right hand.)[57]

Since one has to put on the *shel yad* first, it should always be placed on the same side of the bag so that one will always take it out first. Some have the *minhag* of wrapping the straps differently around the *shel rosh* and the *shel yad*. These reminders are necessary so that we do not mistakenly take out the *shel rosh* first.[58] Even so, if a person accidentally touched or took out the *shel rosh* first, he should *not* put it on. Instead, he should put it back and take out the *shel yad*.[59]

Because of the love for the mitzvah, it is the *minhag* to kiss the tefillin when taking them out and putting them back into their bag.[60]

Be sure not to hang or carry the tefillin by the straps.[61] Even when the tefillin are inside the bag, care should be taken not to carry the bag by the corner with the fingers lest they fall to the ground, *chas v'shalom*. Instead, they should be carried securely underneath the bag or firmly held by the hand against the chest.

When a person leaves his home for an overnight trip, he should take along his tefillin so that he will have them to wear the next morning.[62]

In the year 1490, Rabbi Yosef Gikatilya, the author of *Shaarei Orah*, became seriously ill and was on the verge of death. Suddenly, he saw before him two men weighing his sins against his merits. When he saw that they equalled one another, he immediately asked that his tefillin be brought to him. As soon as he put them on, he started to feel better and, not long thereafter, fully regained his health.

Various stages in the making of the *shel rosh* in *gassoth* tefillin.

Various stages in the making of the *shel yad*.

Kanfe yona: various ways of winding the straps around the *bayith* to resemble the wings of a dove. The middle one is the most common way. (Note that the knot is placed on top instead of underneath the *bayith*.)

[9] HOW MANY BERACHOTH ARE MADE? MUST ONE STAND WHEN PUTTING ON TEFILLIN?

The number of *berachoth* which are made on tefillin is a complicated question dating from the time of the *Gemora* and depends today on *minhag*.[63] Most say two *berachoth*, "...*lahaw-niach tefillin* [לְהָנִיחַ תְּפִילִין] on the *shel yad* and "...*al mitzvath tefillin*" [עַל מִצְוַת תְּפִילִין] on the *shel rosh*. Others say only the first beracha – the custom common among Sephardim and some Chassidic communities.

Special care must be taken not to talk between putting on the *shel yad* and the *shel rosh*.[64] This rule applies no matter if one or two *berachoth* are recited. Pretend that you are swimming under water; would you dare try to breathe in air at a time like that? Indeed, one should not even answer *kaddish* or *kedusha*; instead, one must stop and listen. We can understand how important this law is when we realize that, in the times of old, a Jewish soldier who failed to keep silent when putting on his tefillin was sent home from the battle front – a sign of grave disgrace.[65]

If one who normally says two *berachoth* did speak before putting on the *shel rosh*, then:

[1] if he answered *amen, kaddish* or *kedusha*, he need only say עַל מִצְוַת on the *shel rosh*;[66]

[2] if he said anything else, then he should recite two *berachoth* on the *shel rosh* – first עַל מִצְוַת, then (after the *shel rosh* is in place) לְהָנִיחַ on the *shel yad*, being sure to

move the *shel yad* slightly.[67] Afterwards, *baruch shem kavod* is said.

Those, however, who normally make one beracha, need to say only עַל מִצְוַת תְּפִילִין on the *shel rosh*.[68]

One should be careful to say *lahawniach* לְהָנִיחַ tefillin, and not *lahahniach* לְהַנִּיחַ tefillin. What a world of difference one vowel sound can make! Instead of saying "...for the placing [לְהָנִיחַ *lahawniach*] of tefillin," one could wrongly say "...for the leaving off [לְהַנִּיחַ *lahahniach*] of tefillin."[69] The first one is spelled with a *kametz* and the second one with a *pasach*. Also, when saying עַל מִצְוַת *al mitzvath tefillin*, be careful not to say עַל מִצְוֺת *al mitzvoth tefillin* since the *shel rosh* is only one mitzvah and not two mitzvoth.

Did you ever wonder why we say *lahawniach* [לְהָנִיחַ] tefillin and not *likshor* [לִקְשׁוֹר] tefillin, which would be more like the *nusach* of the *posuk*, וּקְשַׁרְתָּם לְאוֹת עַל יָדְךָ? One commentator points out that originally the mitzvah was to wear tefillin all day long.[70] Had *likshor*, to bind, been used, we might have thought that the mitzvah was fulfilled simply by wearing them for an instant. לְהָנִיחַ, on the other hand, implies placing them on for a longer period of time.

For those who say two berachoth, the second beracha is said only after the *shel rosh* is placed on the head. When saying the beracha one should be sure that his yarmulke is on his head. Now, one should carefully press down the straps tightly around one's whole head, making certain that:

[1] the black of the straps is showing;

[2] the *bayith* is centered on the hair-line, "between the eyes" (see Diagrams 4 and 5);

[3] the knot is centered in the back of the head (see Diagram 9).

Then, only *after* one is certain that his tefillin and straps are adjusted, should he say "*baruch shem kavod malchutho l'olam va'ed.*"[71]

Many ask: why do we say *baruch shem kavod* after saying the beracha *al mitzvath tefillin* on the *shel rosh*? If a person makes a mistaken beracha, he says *baruch shem kavod*. But, here in tefillin, the second beracha is required for Ashkenazim. So why do we say *baruch shem kavod*?

The *Mishna Berura* explains that the second beracha is necessary, but we say *baruch shem kavod* only as an extraordinary measure to remove all shadow of doubt [לרווחא דמלתא] since there are some authorities who do not require the second beracha.[72]

Many people mention the names of the four *parshiyoth* as part of the *tefillah* (*l'shem yechud*) which is recited before laying tefillin. Indeed, it is important to say this prayer since it can increase one's *kavannah*, and *Chazal* have taught us that the mitzvah of serving HaShem "with all your heart" (*Devorim* 11:13) includes preparing your *kavannah* before you do a mitzvah.[73]

If a person has to go to the bathroom during *davening*, he should remove his tefillin and, when he returns, he should put them on with a beracha.[74]

The knot should be centered on the back of the head at the base of the skull but still on the bone. Not too high and not too low, not to the right and not to the left (see Diagram 9).

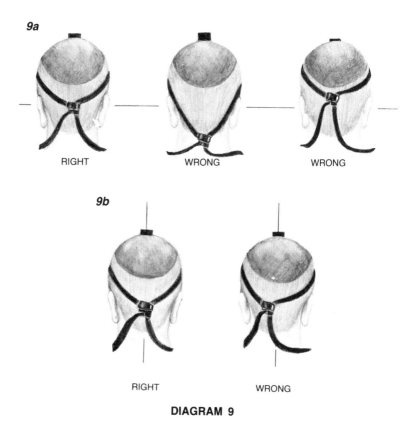

9a

RIGHT   WRONG   WRONG

9b

RIGHT   WRONG

DIAGRAM 9

These exact positions have symbolic meaning. On the bone in the back of the head and not in the hollow of the neck points out that Israel should be on top and not on the bottom (see

Diagram 9a). Directly opposite the front of the face and not on the sides hints that Israel should be in front and not in back (see Diagram 9b). The Maharsha explains that the crown of Torah mentioned in *Pirke Avoth* (4:17) applies to the tefillin *shel rosh*.[76] Therefore, "being on top" indicates that the Jewish People will be supreme through Torah; and "being in front" refers to a Jew with the crown of Torah coming before the crowns of *Kehunah* and *Malchuth*.

The *minhag* among most communities is to stand when putting on tefillin and when taking them off. The Sephardic community is a major exception since its custom is to sit while putting on the *shel yad*.[77]

[10] ARE STRAPS OF THE TEFILLIN ABSOLUTELY NECESSARY? MUST THEY ALSO BE BLACK? HOW MANY TIMES IS THE STRAP WOUND AROUND THE ARM? THE PERMANENT KNOTS OF THE *SHEL ROSH* AND THE *SHEL YAD* LOOK LIKE WHICH HEBREW LETTERS?

A kite without a string is still a kite, but tefillin without their straps are not kosher tefillin. Why?

Since the Torah tells us to *bind* on ourselves the tefillin, we understand that by simply balancing one on the head and pressing the other against the arm we are not fulfilling the mitzvah of binding. Therefore, straps – called *retzuoth* – are an essential part of the mitzvah and are one of the eight laws of tefillin listed by the Rambam as *halacha l'Moshe m'Sinai.*[78]

Still, "binding" implies making a knot to tie something securely. But the knots of the *shel yad* and *shel rosh* are permanent, and all that we do is tighten the straps on our arm and head. *Chazal* have explained, however, that this tightening is all that is necessary to fulfill the words of the Torah, "to bind them."[79]

The *retzuoth* are made from the hide of a kosher animal. If this seems obvious to you by now, then listen to this true story from the time of Rabbi Akiva.[80] Once, one of Rabbi Akiva's students came into the *Beth HaMidrash* wearing tefillin with straps made of blueish wool which was obviously against the *halacha.* The student, however, must have been unaware of this law. Rabbi Akiva did not say anything to him. His fellow *chachamim* wondered how such a *tzaddik* like Rabbi Akiva could allow this mistake. But then they realized that he, in fact, had not seen the student, for had he seen him, Rabbi Akiva surely would have told him the proper *halacha.* We see from this story, interestingly, that under normal circumstances the teacher is held responsible for his student's shortcomings and mistakes.

It is *halacha l'Moshe m'Sinai* that the *retzuoth* must be colored black on the outside. The *Mishna Berura* warns us that if the black paint fades or chips off, it must be repainted.[81] Not any black paint will do; so do not go down into your father's workshop looking for any regular black paint. Instead, show the tefillin to a rabbi or take them directly to a tefillin-maker to touch them up.

Further, painting the straps black, like many other steps in the making of tefillin, must be done specifically for the purpose of fulfilling the mitzvah of tefillin, לִשְׁמָה. Make sure that the place where the *shel yad* is tightened is completely black since pulling the strap makes it likely that the paint will wear off. The width of the *retzuah* is the length of a barley grain, which according to the Chazon Ish is eleven millimeters (slightly under half an inch) and according to Rabbi A.C. Na'eh is ten millimeters (.39 inch).[82]

When wearing tefillin, one should be very careful that only the black side of the strap shows. This rule applies (1) along the circumference of the head and (2) along the first complete turn turn of the *retzuah* closest to the *bayith* on the *shel yad*.[83] Of course, it is best to have the whole length of the *retzuoth* showing on the black side.

The right strap of the *shel rosh* should extend at least until the waist while the minimum length of the left strap is down to the chest.[84] The custom today is to have both straps extend at least to the navel (*tabor*). This hints to how far the influence of the mitzvoth affect this world – until the very core (*tabor*, i.e., center of the earth); and not like some who say that HaShem's influence only reaches down to the moon (i.e., celestial influences).[85]

When putting on the *shel yad*, most people wind the *retzuah* seven times on the arm from the elbow to the wrist. They stop at the wrist because many *poskim* hold that the mitzvah of the *shel yad* does not extend beyond this point. Then they put on the *shel rosh* and, afterwards, return to wind the *retzuah* of the *shel yad* three times around the middle finger (see Diagram 10).

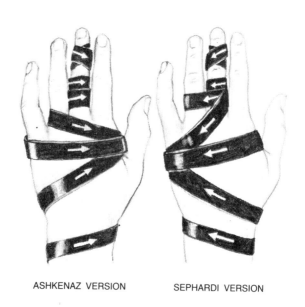

ASHKENAZ VERSION   SEPHARDI VERSION

DIAGRAM 10

The knot of the *shel rosh* is shaped into the letter *dalet* [ד] and the knot of the *shel yad*, into the letter *yud* [י] (see photographs, p.49). Although some have the *minhag* of making two *dalets* for the *shel rosh* one inside the other, the *Mishna Berura* suggests that one *dalet* is preferable.[86] Since the *yud*-knot of the *shel yad* should be tight against the *bayith*, a sinew thread is sometimes used to hold it against the *bayith*.[87]

[11] WHAT ARE THE *TITURA* AND THE *MA'ABARTA*?

The *titura*, an Aramaic word meaning "bridge," is the name given to the base of the tefillin, and like the *bayith*, is made of leather and painted black. The mitzvah *min hamuvchar* is to have the *bayith, titura* and *ma'abarta* all made together from a single piece of leather.[88]

Extending from the *titura* is the *ma'abarta*, which has this name because the strap passes (*ma'abar*) through it (see Diagram 11). It is considered separate from the *titura* since the

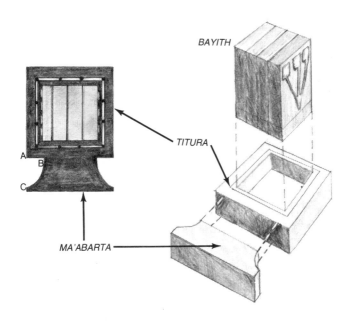

DIAGRAM 11

titura is required to be perfectly square. Therefore, from the edge of the *titura* to the back of the *ma'abarta*, the leather is cut out in the shape of a semi-circle (see points A–B–C) to show that it is not part of the *titura*.

Both the *titura* and the *ma'abarta* are *halacha l'Moshe m'Sinai*, and tefillin without them are not considered kosher.[89]

In *dakoth* and *peshutim* tefillin, a square hole is cut in the upper "tongue" of the *titura*, and a separately made *bayith* with flaps is squeezed through the hole, the flaps remaining between the upper and lower "tongues" of the *titura* (see Diagram 12).

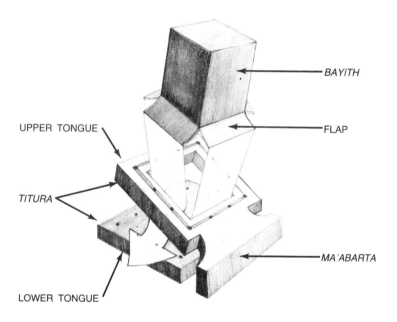

UPPER TONGUE

TITURA

LOWER TONGUE

BAYITH

FLAP

MA'ABARTA

DIAGRAM 12

Next, the *titura* is closed tight and sewn together with a sinew thread, special care being taken that the thread goes through the flaps of the *bayith* as well (see also photographs p. 34, showing stages in the making of *gassoth* tefillin).

Just as the *batim* must be made by an expert tefillin-maker, so the *parshiyoth* must be written by a reliable *sofer*. The laws of writing *S'TaM* are very intricate and numerous, and even a slight mistake in one letter can invalidate the whole *parsha*. Therefore, when purchasing tefillin, one should investigate the *kashruth* of both the *batim* and the *parshiyoth*.[89a]

In all types of tefillin, before the *titura* is sewn together the *parshiyoth* are rolled up and tied with calf's hair, covered with a piece of parchment (*matlith*) and then tied again. And as we see from the following story, sometimes even more can go into the *titura*:

Zev, son of the Admor Rebbe Michel of Zalotshov, was not distinguished in his youth by his scholarship or outstanding character. A few months before his Bar Mitzvah, his father asked the *sofer* to bring him the *parshiyoth* before placing them in the tefillin. When the *sofer* brought them, Rebbe Michel took the *bayith*, turned it upside down and opened up the "tongues" of the *titura* in order to look inside. Suddenly, with tremendous emotion, he broke into tears and just kept crying and crying. The tears rolled down his cheeks and into the *bayith*. Only after it was filled with tears did the Admor stop crying. He emptied the tears and let the tefillin dry out thoroughly. Then, he carefully put the *parshiyoth* into the tefillin and told the *sofer* to have the "tongues" sewn together.

On the day of his Bar Mitzvah, the Admor's son Zev put on the tefillin for the first time. Immediately, he felt the spirit of HaShem enter him and change him and, right then and there, vowed to dedicate his life to the service of HaShem and his fellow man.

[12] CAN TEFILLIN BE WORN AT NIGHT? WHY ARE THEY NOT WORN ON SHABBAT AND YOM TOV? WHEN ARE TEFILLIN FIRST WORN?

According to most authorities, any time, day or night, weekday, Shabbat and Yom Tov, the Torah permits the wearing of tefillin. Why, then, do we not wear them at night or on Shabbat and Yom Tov? *Chazal* have answered this question in detail.[90]

Sleeping with tefillin on is forbidden since we cannot control our passing gas, which is forbidden when wearing tefillin. Since the onset of darkness is the beginning of sleep-time, the *Rabbonim* forbade wearing tefillin at nighttime.

One commentator cites a scriptural allusion to help us understand why passing gas is not permitted.[91] It says in *Tehillim* (49:21), "A man who is in honor and understands not is like the beasts that perish." *Chazal* call tefillin "honor" as it says in *Esther* (8:16), "The Jews had light, and gladness, and joy, and honor." "Honor," says the *Gemora* in *Megilla* 16b, refers to tefillin. Passing gas is the animal part of us and is not proper while wearing tefillin. Now we can re-read the *posuk* in *Tehillim*: "A man who is in honor because he is wearing tefillin and does not understand the law about not passing gas is like the non-understanding beasts that perish."

When is nighttime for the purposes of this prohibition? If the sun has just set and we have not yet laid tefillin, we are still permitted to put them on, but without a beracha.[92] However, after the stars have come out, we are no longer able to put them on.

Before dawn is also considered nighttime. At a certain period after dawn, when "one can recognize a casual friend at a distance of four *amoth*," even though the sky is barely light, we may put on tefillin and make the *berachoth*.[93] During the winter when the sun rises late, it is permitted to put on tefillin before dawn provided that it is impossible to do so later. However, one should say the *berachoth* only after dawn, also moving the tefillin slightly. If a beracha was mistakenly made while it was still night, a second beracha is not necessary.[94]

There are two reasons which *Chazal* give for not wearing tefillin on Shabbat and Yom Tov. Just as two witnesses are needed to establish a fact in Jewish courts, a Jew needs two signs or witnesses to show that he is truly living his Jewishness. On weekdays, the two witnesses are tefillin ("it shall be for you as a sign") and *brith milah* ("the sign of the holy covenant"). Shabbat and Yom Tov are also called signs, as it says, "between Me and the Children of Israel, it [Shabbat] shall be an eternal sign.''[95] Therefore, tefillin are not necessary on these days since the sign of Shabbat and Yom Tov replaces the sign of tefillin.

One could ask what is wrong with having all three signs together. And the answer is that the sign of tefillin would be cheapened (זלזול לאות) by the already existing sign of Shabbat.[96] In addition, tefillin are forbidden on Shabbat because one might accidentally go outside with them on and be guilty of moving an object from one domain to another.[97]

We can also give a third answer from a different approach. Tefillin are one of the signs of a Jew. They are a daily reminder of our obligations and special closeness to HaShem. As one of the first mitzvoth of the day, tefillin can have an effect on us for the whole day. Shabbat and Yom Tov are also reminders of our obligations and closeness to HaShem. Special *davening* and the Torah reading in shul, festive meals, singing *zemiroth* around the table are all strong, visible signs of being a Jew. Therefore, on these days we do not need the sign of tefillin to remind us of our Yiddishkeit.

On *Chol HaMoed*, the *minhag* in *Eretz Yisroel* is not to wear tefillin, even privately. In *Chutz L'aretz*, however, many follow the Rama's halachic decision and wear tefillin.[98]

Tefillin are required to be worn at age thirteen, but various *minhagim* determine how long before age thirteen the young man practices wearing tefillin. Most begin about a month or two before the Bar Mitzvah while some wait until the Bar Mitzvah day

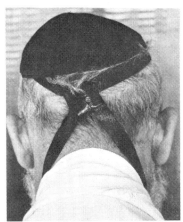

The *dalet*-knot of the *shel rosh*. Left: single *dalet*; right: double *dalet*.

Close-up of single *dalet*-knot (left) and *yud*-knot (right).

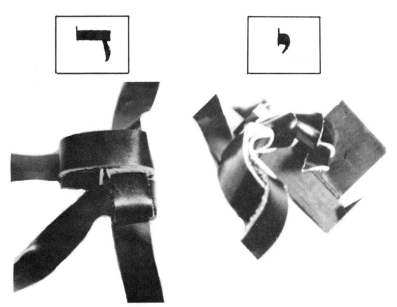

itself.[99] Moroccan Jews are unique; they start a year before the Bar Mitzvah!

Why are there such differences in *minhagim*? And why is there not a mitzvah of *chinuch* by tefillin? Young boys put on *tzitzits* and take the *lulav*, but we do not train them early in tefillin. Why not?

The *Gemora* is *Succah* 42a says that once a child can reliably watch over tefillin, he can begin wearing them. "Watching over tefillin" means not going into the bathroom while wearing them, not sleeping with them on, and not passing air while having them on – the concept of *guf naki* (clean body). Since a child is not able to maintain a *guf naki*, there is no mitzvah of *chinuch*. Only as he approaches his Bar Mitzvah is he considered mature enough to control himself, with different *minhagim* exactly how much before age thirteen.

[13] WHY IS THE LETTER *SHIN* FOUND ONLY ON THE *SHEL ROSH*? HOW MANY TIMES? CAN IT BE SIMPLY PAINTED ON? WHY DOES ONE *SHIN* HAVE FOUR HEADS?

The Hebrew letter *shin* surely must be a very special letter to be found on the tefillin not just once but twice. What makes it so unique a letter that it gets double honor over twenty-one other letters?

The *shin* in tefillin is *halacha l'Moshe m'Sinai* and is made in the leather of the *shel rosh* itself.[100] On the right side of the one wearing tefillin is a three-headed *shin*, and on his left side is a four-headed *shin*. The *shin* should touch the *titura* and is *mihudar* if shaped like the *shin* in the *Sefer Torah*.[101]

It is not kosher halachically simply to paint on a *shin* or to glue on a piece of leather cut out in the shape of a *shin*. Usually a metal stencil-molded type *shin* is placed on the outside and set under pressure until the soft leather bulges out in the form of a *shin*[102] (see photographs, p. 30).

Although there are many reasons why there are two *shins*, why one has four heads and why they are on the *shel rosh*, we will offer just a few.

The two *shins* hint to the 613 mitzvoth.[103] How? The *gematria* of each *shin* is 300, and two *shins* make 600. The two *shins* spell the word *shesh* [שש] six, giving us 606. The number of heads on each *shin* is three and four, which together are seven. 606 plus seven is 613, indicating the *Taryag mitzvoth*.

The four-headed *shin* hints to the script used in the original Tablets from *Har Sinai*.[104] The letters of the Tablets were bored all the way through the stone. Therefore, the *shin* used on the Tablets had three hollowed-space heads, but for us to allude to this *shin*, we make four heads because that leaves three spaces in between – like the way that it was found in the Tablets (see Diagram 13).

Why are the *shins* on the *shel rosh*? When we recall the *posuk*, "And all the peoples of the earth shall see that the name of the L-rd is called upon you; and they shall be afraid of you" (*Devorim* 28:10), and how *Chazal* tell us that this refers to the

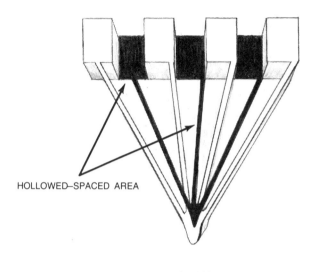

HOLLOWED–SPACED AREA

DIAGRAM 13

tefillin *shel rosh*, an obvious question arises. How in fact does the *posuk* teach us of the *shel rosh*?

Listen carefully to the answer. The four letter Name of Hashem in *aat-bash** spells *matz-patz* [מצפ״״ץ].[105] The *gematria* of these four letters is 40, 90, 80, and 90, which add up to 300. Therefore, the letter *shin* on the *shel rosh* which all the world can see will cause every one to be in awe since the *shin* (300) hints to the name of HaShem.

---

* *aat-bash* is a method of interchanging letters. The first letter of the Hebrew alphabet is replaced by the last letter , *alef* for *toph* (aa't א–ת), the second with the next to last, *beth* for *shin* (ba'sh ב–ש), and so on.

Why is the four-headed *shin* on the left side of the one who is wearing tefillin? Actually, this *shin* is on the right side of anyone facing the wearer of tefillin. One commentator explains that HaShem is the one who is facing us, as it says in *Tehillim* 16:8, "I have set the L-rd always before me."[106] Therefore, the four-headed *shin* of the Tablets is on His right side, the side which represents special holiness, as it says, "from His right hand went a fiery law for them" (*Devorim* 33:2).

The two *shins* spell the word *saas* [שָׂשׂ], joy.[107] The mitzvah of tefillin is a joy and an honor. To show us how high tefillin can bring a person who understands what he is really wearing, *Chazal* tell us the following story:[108] Once when Abaye was together with Rabba, he noticed Rabba in an exhilarated state of great joy. Abaye cautioned him: "Should we not be careful lest we become overjoyous and light-headed, as it says, '...and rejoice with trembling' (*Tehillim* 2:ll)?" Rabba turned to him with a gentle smile and replied: "I just put on my tefillin which are a witness that I have my Master's task before me to do. Although I am rejoicing because I am wearing Tefillin, the tefillin are also safeguarding me from becoming light-headed."

Tefillin are a precious gift from HaShem to each and every one of us. The very name of *Sha–Kai, shin–dalet–yud* is spelled out on us every time we put them on.[109] So let us involve ourselves in seriously studying the laws of tefillin and in understanding their meaning and holiness. For then we can use each morning of our lives to feel closer to HaShem and, thereby, give the whole day greater joy and purpose. Tefillin are a firm ladder upon which we can climb up and up in our service of the Almighty.[110] Now it is up to us to work hard and strive to achieve their potential. *B'hatzlacha*!

A tefillin-maker at work.

APPENDIX I

Practical Guide: How to put on Tefillin

Note: Numbers in brackets refer the reader back to "Answers with Explanations."

1. Take out the tefillin *shel yad* first, leaving the *shel rosh* in the bag and unravel the strap [8]. It is necessary to have in mind the purposes tefillin, which are to proclaim the unity of HaShem and to remember His taking us out of Egypt. Therefore, many are accustomed to say the *l'shem yechud* before putting on the *shel yad* [9]. It is customary, as well, to kiss the tefillin now when taking them out and later when putting them back [8].

2. While still standing (except for Sephardim), a right-handed person should place the *shel yad* on the middle of the biceps muscle of his left arm, slightly tilting the *bayith* towards the heart. A left-handed person should place it on his right arm [4]. Some take off the protective cardboard cover until after saying *baruch shem kavod* [6].

3. Before actually tightening the strap, one should carefully

and thoughtfully say the beracha of ...*lahawniach* לְהָנִיחַ tefillin [9].

4. Without speaking, one tightens the strap at the *bayith*, being careful that the black side is showing and nothing (e.g., shirt sleeve) is under the *bayith*. Then one winds it seven times down to the wrist and temporarily ties the rest around the palm of his hand [10]. The shirt sleeve may be pulled down over the *bayith* at this time.

5. Next, while remaining absolutely silent, one takes the *shel rosh* out of the bag and places it on his head. Some have the *minhag* of first looking at the two *shins* and kissing the knot. If he follows the custom of making two *berachoth*, he now says "...*al mitzvath* עַל מִצְוַת tefillin" and only then centers and tightens it down on his head, being careful both to center the knot of the *shel rosh* and to keep the black side of the straps showing. (Remember that the knot should be on the bone at the back of the head just above the hollow leading to the neck.) Immediately thereafter, one says *baruch shem kavod malchutho l'olam va'ed* [5,9,10]. Then one makes sure that the two straps come down in front of his body.

6. Now one unwraps the strap around his palm and winds it three times around the middle finger while reciting the *posukim* in Hoshea (2:21-22), "And I will betroth you to Me for ever..." [10]. (See Diagram 10 for several ways to wrap the middle finger.)

7. One should touch the tefillin regularly, especially when

reciting the *Kiriyath Shema*, "and you shall bind them as a sign on your hand, and they shall be as frontlets between your eyes" [5].

8. After the *davening* is completed, before removing the *shel rosh*, one should stand up and unwind the strap from around the fingers and wind this part again around his palm. Using his weaker hand, one should carefully remove the *shel rosh*, enclose it in its special case, wrap up the straps on each side, and return it to the bag [8]. As mentioned, it is customary to kiss the tefillin.

9. Then one unwinds the strap from his palm and arm, loosening the bond at the *bayith* in order to remove the *shel yad*.

10. Finally, one encloses the *shel yad* in its case, wraps the strap around and returns it to the bag, being sure always to place it on one particular side. In this way, the next time one puts on tefillin, he will know exactly which side to reach for the *shel yad* first without touching the *shel rosh* [8].

APPENDIX II

Practical Guide: What happens if...?

TAKING OUT THE TEFILLIN

1. If one starts to take the *shel rosh* instead of the *shel yad*, even inside the bag:

    Leave go of the *shel rosh* and proceed to take out the *shel yad*.

2. If, *chas v'shalom*, they should drop on the floor with their protective cases:

    The *minhag* is to give charity instead of fasting. Obviously, they should be picked up right away and kissed. Check to make sure that they were not damaged, especially the top corners of the *bayith*.

3. If both are taken out by mistake:

    Return the *shel rosh* into the bag.

SHEL YAD

1. If one forgot to say the beracha until after he finished winding the strap down to the wrist:

    Say the beracha and then move the *bayith* slightly back and forth.

2. If one realized, after making the beracha, that the *bayith* was

not in the proper position (for instance, it was too close to the elbow or it was facing out instead of toward the heart):

He should adjust it now – it is still part of the mitzvah of *shel yad* – without speaking. The beracha is not repeated.

3. If the *yud*-knot is not firmly against the *bayith*:

See p. 42.

4. When a left-handed person borrows a pair of tefillin from someone who is right-handed (or vice versa), should he change the knot?

No. It is sufficient to turn the *bayith* upside-down (i.e., with the *ma'abarta* towards the hand).

5. If one has a watch on his wrist:

One is not required to remove it although the custom is to do so.

THE BERACHA

1. Just when one is about to make the beracha להניח, and everything is in place, the *chazan* starts *kaddish*:

Wait and do not say the beracha until after he has finished *kaddish*. Obviously, one should answer *kaddish*.

2. When saying the beracha להניח, one forgot to say "who has sanctified us by His mitzvoth and commanded us..."; that is, one said, :ברוך אתה ה' אלקינו מלך העולם – להניח תפילין

One is not יוצא and must repeat the beracha.

3. By mistake, one says על מצות תפילין on the *shel yad* instead of להניח תפילין:

> If one's *minhag* is to say one beracha, then one need not do anything; he is יוצא.
>
> If one's *minhag* is to say two berachoth, then:
>
> (a) if one realizes his mistake right away, before tightening the knot, he should say the proper beracha immediately.
>
> (b) after tightening the knot, however, some authorities hold that one should say להניח on the *shel rosh* while other authorities hold that no beracha is necessary on the *shel rosh*. *L'halacha*, one should say להניח.

BETWEEN *SHEL YAD* AND *SHEL ROSH*

1. Before putting on the *shel rosh*, someone accidentally spoke — even one word:

> Put on the *shel rosh* and say על מצות (this applies even to those people whose *minhag* is not to say a beracha on the *shel rosh*), and then after the *shel rosh* is in place, those who say two berachoth should say להניח on the *shel yad*, moving the *bayith* slightly back and forth.

2. Should one answer *kaddish, kedusha* and *amen* before putting on the *shel rosh*?

> See p. 35.

3. Can one motion to someone else, point to something, or signal in any way in response to someone else?

It is better not to unless it is directly connected with the mitzvah of tefillin. There should be as short a time-lapse as possible between the *shel yad* and the *shel rosh*.

4.   One has to go to the bathroom:

Take off the *shel yad* and cover it. After returning, put it on again with a beracha. (See "Notes" 74, for dis-cussion of how various situations alter the *halacha*.)

SHEL ROSH

1.   *Kaddish* is begun just as one is about to put on the *shel rosh*. Should one wait or should one finish putting it on as fast as possible (i.e., say the beracha – if it is one's *minhag* – and move the bayith to the middle of the hairline) so that one can answer *kaddish*?

Yes, if one is sure not to forget all these essential steps.

2.   After the beracha was said, the *bayith* was not moved back and forth and centered (because it had already been centered before making the beracha):

According to most authorities the beracha on the *shel rosh* was לבטלה – a beracha said in vain. Therefore, extreme care should always be taken to say the beracha while the *shel rosh* is approximately centered on the head. After the beracha is said, it should be accurately centered with its knot on the bone in the back of the head, and then the straps around the head should be pressed down firmly. Only then is *baruch shem kavod* said.

3. The unpainted sides of the straps are left showing:

(a) Along the circumference of the head: it is required to reverse the straps.

(b) From the knot down: it is not required to do so, but it is better if possible. If "(a)" is not discovered immediately, the *minhag* is to give charity. (This custom also applies to the *shel yad* for the first winding around the arm.)

4. While pressing down the straps around the head, one realizes that the knot lies below its proper place. Which is better: to have the *bayith* extend over the hair-line slightly on the forehead (so that the knot is in its proper place), or to have the knot lower (so that the *bayith* is in its proper place)?

The knot should be lower, but not so low as to be on the neck where there is no hair. Later the knot should be readjusted.

DURING DAVENING

1. One has to leave to go to the bathroom:

Take off the tefillin in the same order as normally done. They do not have to be wrapped up in their boxes, but something should be placed over them, such as the tefillin bag. Afterwards, put them on with a beracha. (See Note 74).

2. If one accidently passed gas:

Be sure never to do it again. If one senses that he will continue to pass gas, the tefillin should be removed. When they are put back on, a beracha must be recited.

3. If the strap on the arm loosens and begins to unravel:
   Wind it again, checking to see that the *shel yad* is in its right place. If the *bayith* moved only slightly, no beracha is required.

TAKING THE TEFILLIN OFF

1. If one unwraps the straps of the *shel yad* all the way to the *bayith* (instead of to the wrist) before taking off the *shel rosh*:
   If the *bayith* is still secure on the arm, then just remove the *shel rosh*.

2. May one speak while taking them off?
   Yes.

3. If one takes off the *shel rosh* without first unwinding the strap around the fingers:
   Be careful next time to first unwrap the strap.

PUTTING THE TEFILLIN AWAY

1. As one winds the strap around the *bayith*, the end of the strap dangles and falls to the floor:
   It should be lifted up immediately (since it is a בזיון מצוה, degrading act).

2. If, *chas v'shalom*, they should drop on the floor *without* their protective cases:
   A rabbi should be consulted.

SOURCES

Taking out:
(1) O.Ch. 25:6, M.B. 23.
(2) *Beth Baruch* 14:77, 223–225;
M.B. 40:3.
(3) O.Ch. 25:6, *Beth Baruch*
13:20.

Shel Yad:
(1) *Maasaf L'Kol HaMachanoth*
25:8, note 60.
(2) *Beth Baruch* 13:52.
(4) Ibid. 14:79.
(5) Ibid. 14:93, in the name of the
Pri Meggadim.

The Beracha:
(1) *pashut.*
(2) Rabbi Sheinberg, *shelita.*
(3) O.Ch. 25:5, *Shaarei Teshuva,*
note 5. *L'halacha,* Rabbi Sheinberg, *shelita.*

Between:
(1) O.Ch. 25:9 Rama, M.B. 32,
Bi'ur Halacha, U'ldidan.

(3) Ibid. Beer Hetev 8.

Shel Rosh:
(1) *pashut.*
(2) O.Ch. 25:5 Rama, M.B. 21.
(3) Ibid. 27:11, M.B. 38.
(4) *Beth Baruch* 14:66.

During:
(1) M.B., O.Ch. 25:12(47).
(2) Ibid., in the name of the *Chayei
Adam.*
(3) O.Ch. 25:12, M.B. 44.

Taking Off:
(1) *pashut.*
(2) *pashut.*
(3) *pashut.*

Putting Away:
(1) *Beth Baruch* 14:196.

APPENDIX III

The proper care of Tefillin

Proper care of tefillin not only increases their life span but also prevents their being disqualified for use. The following are the two major areas where special attention should be given:

Protect from extreme conditions

The two worst enemies of tefillin are heat and water. Within minutes they may cause damage such as warpage and flaking off of the paint. Therefore, never leave tefillin in direct sunlight, on radiators, in the trunk of a car, in the luggage section of an airplane, or on a window sill. One's hair should be absolutely dry before putting on the *shel rosh*.

Beware: although the plastic tefillin bag is good protection against wetness, it does increase the temperature inside the bag.

Prevent rounding of the corners

Try not to hold the corners directly. Instead, handle the tefillin from the *titura*. Make sure that the protective cases are the proper size. If the case is too large, the tefillin will rattle inside. And a case which is too small will cause excessive friction when removing and inserting the tefillin.

Shel Rosh: One of the most dangerous moments in the care of the *shel rosh* is when sliding them in and out of the protective cases. Be careful to pull the tefillin slowly *straight* out of the case even if you are in a hurry. The same applies after *davening* when returning it into the case. Also, when bowing or bending over, take into consideration your distance from the wall, *shtender*, etc.

Shel Yad: Although the danger of sliding them in and out of the protective cases is not as severe as with the *shel rosh*, you should still be just as careful. Also avoid using a shirt sleeve that is too tight, for it will rub on the top of the *bayith*. Always keep the special cardboard cover on.

NOTES

(Some of the abbreviations used below: O.Ch.= *Orech Chaim*, M.B.= *Mishna Berura*, Tos.= *Tosefoth*, Men.= *Menachoth*)

1. Tos. Men. 34b brings the first definition; Yaakov Emden Siddur p. 28 brings the second definition. See Rashi and Hirsch on *Bereishith* 48:11. The *Pri Meggadim* suggests that the root might be *paleh*, to separate (us from the other nations). The *Aruch*, however, maintains that the word tefillin is Aramaic in origin, coming from the root *tafel*, to unite, to join together. Still another use of *pilel* is found in *Yoma* 87a (to pacify).

2. Tos. Men. 34b, which also gives another definition of "looking at."

3. Ibid., *Devorim* 28:10. See Rabbenu Bachaya's commentary on this verse.

4. See Ramban in *Shemoth* 13:16 who explains how tefillin are a *zikaron* (remembrance) (as stated in his commentary to *Shemoth* 13:9):

    "...we are to lay them [tefillin] at the place of remembrance, which is between the eyes, at the beginning of the brain. It is there that remembrance begins by recalling the appearances of persons and events after they have passed away from us. These frontlets (*totofoth*) circle around the whole head with their straps, while the knot rests directly over the base of the brain which guards the memory."

5. *Mitzvath Tefillin*, Shelah HaKodesh, pp. 63-64, *Ohr Tzaddikim*, p.5.
6. *Devorim* 6:4, corresponding to the third letter of HaShem's Name.
7. Ibid. 11:13, corresponding to the fourth letter.
8. *Shemoth* 13:1, corresponding to the first letter.
9. Ibid. 13:11, corresponding to the second letter.
10. See *Berachoth* 14b.
11. Based on commentary of Rabbi Velvel Heshen, *shelita*, Jerusalem.
12. O.Ch. 25:5, M.B. 15.
13. *Devorim* 6:7.
14. *Shemoth* 13:9. See *Kiddushin* 35a.
15. *Mitzvath Tefillin*: Shelah HaKodesh, pp. 64-65. Cf., *Chayei Adam* 14:27 and the explanation of the *Beth Baruch* 249.
16. See his commentary to *Shemoth*, pp. 164-165.
17. See Rashi, *Bereishith* 25:31.
18. The disagreement between Rashi and Rabbenu Tam is based on differing interpretations of a *Braiytah* discussed in the *Gemora*. See Men. 34b.
19. O.Ch. 32:44, M.B. 212.
20. Men. 36b.
21. Ibid. 37a.
22. Ibid.
23. O.Ch. 27:1.
24. Men. 37a.
25. Ibid. 37b.
26. O.Ch. 27:11 (Rama).
27. See M.B. 27:11 (47).
28. Men. 37b.
29. *Devorim* 11:18.
30. O.Ch. 27:1-2 (M.B. 9).
31. Ibid. 27:7, M.B. 18, 29.
32. Ibid. 27:4, M.B. 14.

33. *Megilla* 24b.

34. *Sanhedrin* 88b, *Kiddushin* 37a.

35. Men. 37a.

36. Ibid. 37b.

37. O.Ch. 27:10, M.B. 36.

38. Cf., *Beth Baruch* 14:65, where he concludes that although the use of a mirror is technically permitted, here the use of one's hand is sufficient (ולא ניתנה תורה למלאכי השרת).

39. Ibid. 28:1, M.B. 3.

40. היסח הדעת (forgetfulness) does not mean that one has to realize every second that he is wearing tefillin. It means that the person is occupied with what he is doing and, at the same time, senses the fear of Heaven. Primarily, light-headedness and joking around are considered היסח הדעת. Cf., M.B. to O.Ch. 44:1 (3).

40a. Men. 37a.

41. See *Ein Yaakov*, Men. 37a, *HaBoneh*.

42. See Question 11, p. 43.

43. O.Ch. 27:4, M.B. 15.

43a. *Aruch HaShulchan*.

44. *Shabbat* 49a, 130a.

44a. *Beth Baruch* 14:34.

45. O.Ch. 32:39, M.B. 176. See also Rambam's commentary to *Mishna Eruvin* 4:8.

46. Ibid. 32:40, M.B. 184; Ibid. 33:3, M.B. 19.

47. Based on *Aterath Zekenim*, O.Ch. 32.

48. *Shabbat* 108a.

49. *Berachoth* 6a.

50. *Divre HaYamim* 17:21.

51. Men. 34b.

52. Ibid.

52a. Ibid. 37a.

53. Eliyahu Rabba, O.Ch. 25:5, note 8.

54. Men. 36a.

55. O.Ch. 25:11.

56. Ibid. 28:2, M.B. 6.

57. Ibid.

58. Ibid. 28:2, M.B. 7; see *Bi'ur Halacha*, beginning *Sh'lo yifgo*.

59. Ibid. 25:6, M.B. 23 explains that the reason we pass over the mitzvah is because the *posuk* clearly states to place the *shel yad* first.

60. Ibid. 28:3.

61. Ibid. 40:1.

62. Ibid. 110:4, M.B. 20.

63. Men. 36a.

64. O.Ch. 25:10, M.B. 35.

65. Men. 36a, *Sotah* 44b.

66. O.Ch. 25:10, M.B. 36, *Bi'ur Halacha, Im shama kaddish*.

67. Ibid. 25:9, M.B. 32, *Bi'ur Halacha, U'ldidan*.

68. Ibid. See *Bi'ur Halacha, V'im hifsik*.

69. Ibid. 25:7, M.B. 24.

70. *Bach*. Brought in *Maasaf L'Kol HaMachanoth* by Rabbi Y.M. Gold, p. 11, note 43.

71. O.Ch. 25:5 Rama, M.B. 21.

72. Ibid. Cf., *Aruch HaShulchan* 25:13 for another answer.

73. Cf., O.Ch. 60:4, M.B. 7.

74. Ibid. 25:12, M.B. 47. If a urinal is used, then no beracha is necessary. Today, some *poskim* are lenient in all cases. Therefore, if a regular bathroom is used to urinate and the door is left partially open, we may be lenient. (Rabbi Sheinberg, *Shelita*)

75. Men. 35b.

76. Maharsha, Men. 35b *Kesher*, *Yoma* 72b *Shelosha ze'erim*, Kid. 66a *Maaseh l'Yani HaMelech*.

77. Based on Kabbalah.

78. Hilchoth Tefillin, 3:1.

79. Men. 35b.

80. Ibid. 35a.

81. O.Ch. 33:3, M.B. 19.

82. Siddur *Minchath Yerushalayim*, p. 424.

83. O.Ch. 27:11, M.B. 38.

84. Ibid. M.B. 41.

85. Eliyahu Rabba 25:5, note 8. Brought in *Mitzvath Tefillin*, p. 123, note 2.

86. O.Ch. 32:52, M.B. 233.

87. Ibid. 27:2, M.B. 10. This *halacha* refers to the time when the tefillin are being worn. Those who want to be *machmir*, adds the *Mishna Berura*, and have the *yud*-knot against the *bayith* even when the tefillin are in their bag, should take the advice of using a thread or an extra piece of leather inserted in the *ma'abarta*. If a thread is used, one must be careful not to pass the thread under the *bayith*. Therefore, it is best to ask a reliable person to tie it. Cf., *Ben Ish Chai*, Parshath Vayera, 15, and *Eshel Avraham*.

88. Ibid. 32:44, M.B. 201.

89. Men. 35a, O.Ch. 32:44.

89a. Organizations such as *Vaad Mishmereth STaM* are available for consultation and provide guidelines to follow in this important area.

90. Ibid. 36 a-b.

91. *Shaarei Teshuva*, O.Ch. 30:2.

92. O.Ch. 30:2, M.B. 3. *Bi'ur Halacha, v'yesh mi.*

93. This period of time varies in different latitudes. In *Eretz Yisroel*, it is approximately 52 minutes before sunrise.

94. See O.Ch. 30:3, M.B. 13.

95. *Shemoth* 31:17. There are different opinions how Yom Tov is called a sign. One opinion is that the first Pesach in *Mitzrayim*, which is called "a sign," is compared to all Yomim Tovim, as it says, "And Moses

declared to the children of Israel the appointed seasons of the L-rd'' (*Vayikra* 23:44). (Brought by M.B., O.Ch. 31:1 [3]). Others compared Yom Tov to Shabbat, since Yom Tov is called Shabbat. The *Pri Meggadim* suggests the source is from the *posuk* "...and let them be for signs and for seasons" (*Bereishith* 1:14).

96. O.Ch. 31:1, M.B. 5.

97. Ibid. 29:1, M.B. 2. Some authorities disagree. See also O.Ch. 31:1 and O.Ch. 308:4.

98. Ibid. 31:2 Rama, M.B. 8. The *Mishna Berura* concludes by saying that it is better not to make a beracha on the tefillin.

99. Ibid. 37:3 Rama says to begin on the day of the Bar Mitzvah. See M.B. 12 and *Bi'ur Halacha, d'Hi Katan*, where he explains why we do not follow here the Rama. Cf., *Oth Chaim V'Shalom*, 37:3, note 5, where he supports the ruling of the Rama.

100. Men. 35a.

101. O.Ch. 32:42, M.B. 191.

102. Even when a metal mold is used, some are careful to have the newly-made *shin* pushed back in completely (or in part) and then pulled out again with a pair of pliers.

103. Olath Tamid, Rabbi S. Houminer, p. 17b; *Mitzvath Tefillin*, Shelah HaKodesh, p. 71.

104. O.Ch. 32:42, Taz 35; Eliyahu Rabba 32, note 65.

105. *Mitzvath Tefillin*, Shelah HaKodesh, p. 45, note 18.

106. Eliyahu Rabba, O.Ch. 25:5, note 8.

107. *Olath Tamid*, p. 17b.

108. *Berachoth* 30b. See the *Ben Ish Chai's* explanation in his book *Ben Y'hoyada*, p. 32b. Cf., *Beth Baruch* 14:96. Also, see Rabbenu Yona's commentary to the *Gemora*.

109. The letter *shin* is on the *bayith* of the *shel rosh*; the *dalet*, in the knot of the *shel rosh*; and the *yud* is in the knot of the *shel yad*.

110. *Sefer HaChinuch*, Mitzvah 421.

Postscript

Everybody feels special when he first starts laying tefillin, and as a result he is very careful with all the rules and customs. Unfortunately, though, after a while we sometimes forget the holiness of what we are doing. To prevent such forgetfulness, Rabbi Yeshaya Heshin, *z"tl*, of Yeshivat Etz Chaim in Jerusalem, used to tell the following true story to all his students when they reached Bar Mitzvah.* And, as will be clear from reading the story, it is not just for Bar Mitzvah young men.

The Power of Tefillin Vanquishes a Plague

The European city of Ostraha was famed for its great Torah scholars and *tzaddikim*, including the Maharsha, the Yeybi Saba (author of *Morah Mikdosh*), and many others.

---

*Taken from Rabbi Heshin's book of Bar Mitzvah discourses, *Divre Yeshaya*, Jerusalem, 1954.

Once a devastating plague ravaged the city, threatening the
lives of the entire population. The Chief Rabbi of the city decreed
a day of fasting and prayer, hoping to arouse the Jewish
community to *teshuva*. Then, once the words of the prophet
would be fulfilled: "Let us search and try our ways and turn back
to the L-rd," perhaps HaShem would save the city. Concerned
also that the cause of the calamity may have been an
irresponsible person, the Chief Rabbi announced that anybody
observing anyone suspicious should immediately inform his
office.

It happened that around the time that the plague began, a
certain Jew stopped coming to his regular *minyan* in the
morning. Everyone assumed that he was praying at some other
shul. Now, however, with the heightened concern of the
townspeople, curiosity was aroused, and two men were sent to
investigate the matter. They followed him around the whole day
but found nothing suspicious in his activities. They resolved,
however, also to spy on him at night. Sure enough, at midnight
they noticed that he lit a candle and made preparations to leave.
He then left his house and walked along the road leading out of
the city. The two men followed after him, taking every precaution
to prevent being noticed.

The man walked until he came to the next town, entered
quietly and vanished from their eyes. The two spies were afraid
to continue further, for who knew what danger lay ahead?
Instead, they returned home and, the next morning, reported
their story to the Chief Rabbi. He also felt that the behavior was

very suspicious but realized that there was insufficient proof.

"Tonight," suggested the Chief Rabbi, "stand watch again by his house, and as soon as he lights a candle, one of you come and inform me. I then will join you, and together we'll follow him and find out exactly what he's doing."

That night, everything happened just as the Chief Rabbi suggested. This time, however, when the man entered the second town, the Chief Rabbi and the two spies steadfastly continued after him.

They followed him until he came to a certain spot at the edge of the town and sat down by the side of an old stone wall. Then he took out a *siddur* from his bag and began saying *tikun chatzoth*, prayers recited over the destruction of the Temple. His voice was mournful and full of passion; his heart seemed to melt as he broke out into tears.

The Chief Rabbi and the two spies stood behind a grove of trees and watched him in utter silence. Their amazement grew when they suddenly heard a second voice, also chanting mournfully. There was only one man, yet they distinctly heard two voices. No matter how intently they listened or how closely they spied out the area, they remained baffled as to the source of this mysterious voice. The sound of the second voice was incomparable in depth of feeling; indeed, they had never heard anything like it.

"It's perfectly clear now," whispered the Chief Rabbi to his companions, "that this man is not a cause for our suspicions. Still, I think that we should wait here to see what he does afterwards. Also, maybe we can learn from where the mysterious voice is coming.''

After the man finished reciting *tikun chatzoth*, he stood up, tied his cloth bag, and set out to return home. He had not gone far along the main road before the three secret observers came out in front of him.

"We have been following you all night," admitted the Chief Rabbi, "suspecting that you were the cause of our city's terrible plague. Now that we have seen that you are a true servant of HaShem, all our suspicions have completely vanished, and we therefore beg your forgiveness."

The man nodded his consent but made no comment.

"May I ask you one small question," continued the Chief Rabbi. "We saw you enter the town alone and recite *tikun chatzoth*; yet we heard two voices lamenting. Please tell us, whose was the second voice?"

The man answered by speaking about other topics, evading the question.

"I order you," said the Chief Rabbi sternly, "as the city's rabbi, to answer. Tell us the truth; whose was the second voice which we heard?"

When the *tzaddik* heard the strong tone of the Chief Rabbi, he confessed, "I have no choice but to reveal the truth.

"For many years now I have been accustomed to mourn over the destruction of the *Beit HaMikdosh*. My prayers caused a special response Above, and I was given a gift from Heaven. *Yirmiyahu HaNavi*, who prophesied at the end of the First

Temple and witnessed its destruction, was sent to me every night. Together, we recite the *tikun chatzoth* and lament. This is the second voice, the voice of *Yirmiyahu*, which you heard."

The three listeners were stunned. After a long moment of silence, the Chief Rabbi decided to question the *tzaddik* further.

"We realize now that you are a man of great merit to be found worthy enough to have *Yirmiyahu HaNavi* come and say *tikun chatzoth* with you. Surely your words have a great effect in Heaven. So, I wonder why you have not seen fit to stop this terrible plague. Or, if that is not in your power, at least the cause of the plague — be it a wicked person or some hidden sin — should be known to you. And if you say you don't know this either, then why haven't you asked *Yirmiyahu HaNavi*?

"And a last question," continued the Chief Rabbi curiously. "Why have you not been *davening* in shul recently?"

The *tzaddik* simply replied to the Chief Rabbi's inquiries by saying that the next day he would *daven* in shul and there he would answer all the questions. Their conversation ended as they entered the city of Ostraha. The night was almost over when they separated and returned to their homes.

After *Shacharith*, the two townsmen who had been with the Chief Rabbi could not restrain themselves from revealing the incredible tale. Soon, the whole city was alive with the news that there lived in their midst a hidden *tzaddik* and, tomorrow morning, he would be *davening* in the Central Synagogue.

Early the next morning the synagogue began to fill up, with everybody from young to old coming to see the *tzaddik*. Soon there was no more room left inside, and late-comers were forced to wait outside in the courtyard of the synagogue.

Expectation grew as the time of *Shacharith* arrived and the hidden *tzaddik* still had not appeared. The Chief Rabbi declared, however, that the morning services should not be delayed.

The congregation began *davening*, and because of the large multitude of people, the prayers echoed with great fervor. This increased intensity only heightened everyone's expectancy. Suddenly, in the middle of *Pesukei Dizimra*, the *tzaddik* arrived. His appearance as he entered the synagogue cloaked in his tallit and wearing tefillin caused great fear to spread among the congregants. Alarm and confusion replaced the passionate prayers; some men even fainted from fright.

The *tzaddik* walked straight to the front of the synagogue without seeming to notice the general panic that was surrounding him. He steadfastly made his way to a place by the front corner wall and quietly began *davening*. Slowly everyone resumed his prayers.

At the conclusion of the morning service, the Chief Rabbi came over to the *tzaddik* and said, "You have added an additional marvel to the extraordinary events of yesterday. Why did fear and confusion fill the congregation? Some fainted from fright, you know.

"Also," he added, "you promised the other night to answer in full all the questions I put before you. If you please, now is the time."

"Why the people reacted to my entrance this morning is

simple," answered the *tzaddik*. "It says in the Torah, 'And all the people of the earth shall see that you are called by the name of the L-rd; and they shall be afraid of you.' *Chazal* interpret this verse as referring to the tefillin *shel rosh*. Therefore, tefillin have a special way of igniting awe and fear. So you see, when I entered the synagogue adorned with tefillin, everybody was afraid. The holiness of tefillin...."

"But we all lay tefillin every day," interrupted the Chief Rabbi, "and yet there is never any reaction like this!"

"The reason," explained the *tzaddik*, "is because I am always extremely careful never to speak *divre chol* while wearing tefillin. Also, I am careful always to treat them with proper respect, such as never walking in an unclean place. Thus, the great *kedusha* of my tefillin has never been reduced. There still remains in them the original quality which *Chazal* express: because of the tefillin all the people of the earth will fear you.

"But," warned the *tzaddik*, "if a person does not properly respect his tefillin, then he diminishes their *kedusha*. By speaking *divre chol*, by being light-headed with others in shul, by even forgetting for a minute that you are wearing them – all these reduce the power of tefillin. True, the mitzvah of wearing tefillin is being fulfilled, but their awesomeness has been lost."

He continued in a somber voice, "You wonder why I have not been coming to shul. The reason is simply because of the way everyone conducts himself in shul. First, people do not guard the *kedusha* of their tefillin, as I explained. Second, they are not cautious in their speech, for quite often I heard even *lashon hara* being spoken. Don't they know that a synagogue is a place of great *kedusha*? I simply was not able to tolerate this type of behavior. Moreover, I was afraid that I might weaken, Heaven forbid, and accidentally be pulled into speaking *divre chol*. Therefore, I stopped coming to *daven* in shul.

"Now," concluded the *tzaddik*, "the cause of the dreadful plague in our city should be clear. People are not careful to refrain from speaking *divre chol* in the synagogue. And they are also careless in how they behave when wearing tefillin.

"If you will see fit to correct these things," he advised, "then the plague will end immediately." After he finished speaking, he left the synagogue with his tallit and tefillin held securely under his arm and was never seen again.

Everyone was dumbfounded as the *tzaddik* left, and soon a steady murmur arose from the congregation. At that point, the Chief Rabbi went up to the *bimah* and proclaimed that every member of the community should attend a general assembly to be held later that same day in the same place in order to hear what the *tzaddik* had said.

When the appointed hour arrived, the synagogue was overflowing with people. The Chief Rabbi entered, and a path was made for him as he walked to the pulpit. He spoke with great emotion, intending to arouse the congregation to the seriousness of the situation. After telling the whole story of the hidden *tzaddik*, he explained about the holiness of the synagogue and the requirement of giving it *kavod*. He continued by describing the *kedusha* of tefillin and the prohibition of speaking *divre chol* while wearing them. Then, dramatically raising his voice, he declared to his entire community, "By failing to follow these holy requirements, we have brought upon ourselves the horrible plague that has gripped our city."

Many of the people broke out into tears, and they all openly admitted their error. They took upon themselves to make a general ordinance. From then on, it was absolutely forbidden for any person to speak *divre chol* in the synagogue. The regulation applied as well to being careful in fulfilling every aspect of *hilchoth* tefillin. Later, they had engraved on a plaque in big letters: STRICTLY FORBIDDEN TO SPEAK *DIVRE CHOL* IN THIS SYNAGOGUE.

The people of Ostraha took their vow seriously, never again speaking *divre chol* in shul. Whenever a stranger came into the synagogue and, not knowing of this ordinance, began asking questions or speaking general conversation, they would not answer him. Instead, they would immediately show him the plaque hanging on the wall and then direct him outside. There, they would speak freely with him about all that was on his mind.

As soon as the people of the city accepted these rules upon themselves, the plague ceased. From that time onward, there was light and rejoicing for the Jews of Ostraha.